REMARKABLE
PEOPLE

Steve
Irwin

by Sheelagh Matthews

Published by Weigl Publishers Inc.
350 5th Avenue, Suite 3304, PMB 6G
New York, NY 10118-0069

Website: www.weigl.com

Library of Congress Cataloging-in-Publication Data

Matthews, Sheelagh.
  Steve Irwin / Sheelagh Matthews.
     p. cm. -- (Remarkable people)
  Includes index.
  ISBN 978-1-59036-649-3 (hard cover : alk. paper) -- ISBN 978-1-59036-650-9 (soft
cover : alk. paper)
  1. Irwin, Steve--Juvenile literature. 2. Herpetologists--Australia--Biography--
Juvenile literature. I. Title.
  QL31.I78M38 2008
  597.9092--dc22
  [B]

                             2006036972

Printed in the United States of America
2 3 4 5 6 7 8 9 0 11 10 09 08

Editor: Leia Tait
Design: Terry Paulhus

Cover: Many people were touched by Steve Irwin's passion for wildlife.

Photograph Credits
Permission to reproduce the Commonwealth Coat of Arms granted by the
Department of the Prime Minister and Cabinet of Australia: page 7 top left.

Every reasonable effort has been made to trace ownership and to obtain
permission to reprint copyright material. The publishers would be pleased to
have any errors or omissions brought to their attention so that they may be
corrected in subsequent printings.

Contents

Who Is Steve Irwin?

Steve Irwin loved animals, especially crocodiles. He was known as the "Crocodile Hunter." Steve rescued crocodiles and other wild animals that were in trouble. He was passionate about wildlife **conservation**. Steve wanted to protect animals and their natural homes. He shared these ideas with others. Steve starred in television shows, wrote books, and made public appearances. He owned and ran Australia Zoo with his wife, Terri. Steve inspired many people. Many of them are continuing the work that he began.

"Crikey! I haven't seen an animal I haven't wanted to kiss!"

Growing Up

Steve Irwin was born on February 22, 1962. His family lived in Essendon, on the outskirts of Melbourne, Australia. Steve had two sisters, Joy and Mandy. Animals were always a big part of his family's life. Steve's parents loved nature and animals. His dad, Bob, studied reptiles, collected snakes, and worked with crocodiles. Steve's mother, Lyn, turned the Irwin home into a kind of wildlife shelter. She cared for every animal she found that was injured or in need of food or a place to stay.

When Steve was 8 years old, the family bought 4 acres (1.6 hectares) of tropical land on Australia's Sunshine Coast. Here, they opened a **wildlife sanctuary** in 1970. The sanctuary was called Beerwah Reptile Park.

The Sunshine Coast is known for its long, sunny days and breathtaking scenery.

Get to Know Australia

COAT OF ARMS

FLAG

FLOWER
Golden Wattle

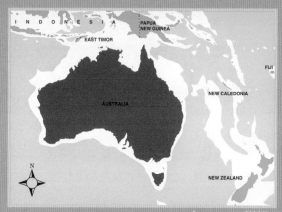

"The outback" is a remote desert area in central Australia.

Canberra is the capital of Australia.

Australia is the world's smallest continent, but is its sixth largest country.

Uluru is a giant red rock in the desert. It is one of the best-known sites in Australia.

There are about 50 million kangaroos in Australia.

Think about it!

Steve was fascinated by Australian wildlife, especially crocodiles. Watch a video, or read a book about your favorite animal. What did you learn? What do you want others to know? Make a poster. Include a photo or drawing of the animal and some interesting facts. Ask your teacher if you can present it to your class.

Practice Makes Perfect

As a young boy, Steve enjoyed taking field trips and working at the reptile park with his dad. Bob was an expert at capturing crocodiles and snakes. Steve wanted to learn to do these things. He watched and copied everything his father did. Under Bob's watchful eye, Steve captured his first crocodile when he was just 9 years old. By the time he was 12, Steve was skilled at catching crocodiles.

After high school, Steve went to North Queensland, Australia. He rescued crocodiles that ventured too close to people. Crocodiles that wandered near populated areas, such as cities or towns, were often hurt or killed. Steve wanted to stop this from happening. He caught many crocodiles and other reptiles that were in danger. These rescues were always exciting and sometimes dangerous. Steve and Bob were trained professionals, or else they would not have attempted these rescues.

▬ Steve's dad, Bob Irwin, invented many of the techniques used by experts to capture snakes and crocodiles today.

Steve was not paid for his rescue work. Instead, he was allowed to relocate each rescued animal to a natural crocodile **habitat** at the family's wildlife sanctuary. There, the crocodiles would be safe.

When he was not busy catching crocodiles, Steve helped his mother care for injured, sick, and stray animals. Lyn often found these animals on the side of the road. Many had been injured by cars. Steve learned a great deal about treating and feeding animals from his mother.

There are both freshwater and saltwater crocodiles in Australia. The saltwater crocodile is the world's largest reptile.

Key Events

Steve met Terri Raines, a young American woman, in 1991. Terri was a wildlife rescue worker and **veterinary nurse**. It was love at first sight for both Terri and Steve. They married the next year. They spent their honeymoon rescuing crocodiles in Queensland.

In 1992, Steve and Terri took over the family reptile park. They renamed it Australia Zoo. That year, Steve's friend John Stainton visited the zoo. John was a television producer. He made a film at the zoo. It was called *The Crocodile Hunter*. The program featured video footage from Steve and Terri's honeymoon adventure. Steve and John decided to make more shows for a television series. *The Crocodile Hunter* aired on the Animal Planet channel in Australia in 1996. One year later, *The Crocodile Hunter* was shown in North America. It was very popular. Through the show, Steve reached millions of people with his message of wildlife conservation.

▓▓ Steve became a father in 1998 when his daughter, Bindi, was born. Steve's son, Bob, was born in 2003.

Thoughts from Steve

Steve loved wildlife, and he often said things that showed how much he cared. Here are some examples.

Steve comes across a crocodile.

"Crikey! Look at this one! What a little beauty!"

Steve describes how people can get along with animals.

"We don't own planet Earth, we belong to it. And we must share it with our wildlife."

Steve encourages wildlife conservation.

"The truth is that we will never save wildlife by killing it. Together, we can work to protect the inhabitants of planet Earth. If we save our wild places, we will ultimately save ourselves."

Steve explains that crocodiles are in danger.

"The single greatest threat is loss of habitat."

Steve loves working with animals.

"Am I the luckiest bloke in the entire world? Yes! I totally believe I am."

Steve describes his approach to teaching others.

"I believe that education is all about being excited about something."

What Is a Conservationist?

A conservationist is someone who protects nature. Conservationists help to protect natural areas or **preserve** habitats. They work to save wildlife or plants. Anyone can be a conservationist. Some people **volunteer** for a conservation cause they care about. Others are paid for the work they perform.

Conservationists take action in many ways. Some rescue wild animals that they treat for injuries or relocate to safer places to live. Others study animals, plants, and habitats to learn more about conservation issues. Conservationists educate the public about what they have learned. They **lobby** governments to protect animals or habitats that are **endangered**. These activities helps conservationists achieve their goals.

To educate people about wildlife conservation, Steve and Terri gave fun and exciting demonstrations.

Conservationists 101

Jane Goodall (1934–)

Interest: Chimpanzee Conservation

Achievements: Dr. Jane Goodall was born in Great Britain. She is a scientist and conservationist. Dr. Goodall is best known for her work with chimpanzees. She studied these animals in their natural habitat. This was in Gombe Stream National Park, in Tanzania, Africa. Her studies lasted many years. Dr. Goodall has received many awards for her conservation work. She works hard to teach others about chimpanzees and the environment. In 1991, Dr. Goodall formed Roots and Shoots, an international program to teach children about the environment.

John Muir (1838–1914)

Interest: Forest Conservation

Achievements: John Muir is one of North America's best-known **naturalists** and conservationists. In the 1870s, Muir urged the U.S. government to protect forests in California. This led to the creation of the Sequoia and Yosemite National Parks in 1890. Two years later, Muir helped found The Sierra Club. The club promoted wilderness outings in the Sierra Nevada Mountains. It brought attention to forest conservation issues. Today, The Sierra Club remains an important environmental group in the United States and Canada.

Sir David Attenborough (1926–)

Interest: Nature Conservation

Achievements: Sir David Attenborough was born in Great Britain. He is recognized worldwide as a naturalist and **broadcaster**. Attenborough was one of the first people to make documentary films about nature. One of his best-known documentary series is called *The Living Planet*. During his long career, Attenborough has received many awards. In 1985, he was knighted by Queen Elizabeth II of Great Britain. There is even a dinosaur named in his honor—*Attenborosaurus conybeari*.

Wangari Maathai (1940–)

Interest: Forest and Soil Conservation

Achievements: Dr. Wangari Maathai is from Kenya, Africa. In 1977, Maathai founded the Green Belt Movement. Her goal was to solve social and environmental problems caused by **deforestation**. She urged Kenya's farmers to plant trees. Planting trees can help stop **erosion**, provide shade, and create a needed source of lumber and firewood for farmers. The Green Belt Movement has expanded to 15 African countries. Farmers across the continent have planted more than 30 million trees. Wangari Maathai won a Nobel Peace Prize in 2004 for her work.

The Documentary

Documentaries are films about real people, places, or things. There are many documentaries about wildlife. Conservationists make documentaries to help others understand why protecting wildlife and the environment is important.

Influences

The person who most influenced Steve was his father, Bob. Steve described Bob as his hero, his **mentor**, and his best friend. Steve wanted to be just like his father. As a child, he followed Bob around and copied everything Bob did. When Steve grew up, he followed in his father's footsteps by becoming a wildlife expert.

Steve's mother, Lyn, also influenced him. Steve learned kindness and patience by helping Lyn care for stray and injured animals. He learned a great deal about animals that were not reptiles. Lyn often cared for kangaroos, possums, and koalas. Helping Lyn greatly improved Steve's wildlife knowledge.

Steve enjoyed working with all types of animals. His experiences as a child helped prepare him for working at Australia Zoo when he grew up.

In the early 1980s, Bob and Lyn decided to try to improve people's negative feelings toward large, saltwater crocodiles. They began educating others about crocodiles. They rescued and relocated crocodiles from public areas. They bought land to preserve as a wildlife habitat. These activities made an impression on Steve. He gladly joined his parents in their work. Conservation became his passion. When he grew up, Steve took over the family's wildlife sanctuary, which is now Australia Zoo. Steve's family continues to own and run Australia Zoo today.

Australia Zoo is one of Queensland's most visited tourist sites.

AUSTRALIA ZOO

Australia Zoo is home to more than 1,000 animals, including koalas, elephants, tigers, birds, and reptiles. The zoo spans more than 60 acres (24 ha) and employs more than 500 people. Each day, thousands of visitors pass through the gates. Australia Zoo staff operate many conservation and education programs. They produce wildlife documentaries and publications. Learn more about the zoo at **www.australiazoo.com.au**.

Overcoming Obstacles

Steve wanted to help people overcome extreme fear of snakes and crocodiles. He wanted people to respect all animals, not just those that are cute and cuddly. To achieve these things, Steve taught people about wildlife and the environment. He performed daring crocodile rescues. He gave thrilling demonstrations at Australia Zoo. Steve carried out new crocodile research aboard his boat, *Croc One*. He tried to make others excited about wildlife.

Steve was not afraid to work with crocodiles and other wild animals. He believed that this would help others learn to respect and understand these animals.

Steve was concerned about the status of crocodiles. Of the 23 **species** of crocodiles in the world, 17 are at risk of becoming **extinct**. Steve worked hard to stop the destruction of crocodile habitats. He started groups that help ensure new communities are built with care and consideration for land that is home to crocodiles. Steve urged people not to buy goods made from crocodile skins, such as boots, belts, or bags.

In his work, Steve frequently came across animals that had been hurt by people. In 2004, he opened the Australian Wildlife Hospital and Rescue Unit, near Australia Zoo. The hospital treats animals that are sick or injured, including victims of human cruelty. Staff also look after young animals that have lost their mothers. They care for the animals until they are ready to be released back into nature.

▓ Veterinarians at the Australian Wildlife Hospital and Rescue Unit treat many koalas that have been injured by cars on Australian roads.

Achievements and Successes

Steve's passion and enthusiasm for wildlife conservation made him a popular television and movie personality. He appeared as a guest many times on *The Tonight Show*, which is hosted by Jay Leno. He also made a brief appearance in the movie *Dr. Doolittle 2*. In 2002, Steve starred in his own full-length movie, *The Crocodile Hunter: Collision Course*.

Steve's hard work is respected and recognized by many. In 2001, he was awarded the Centenary Medal for his service to global conservation and to Australian tourism. Steve also received the Special Award for Contribution to Australia Tourism in 2006.

On *The Tonight Show*, Steve delighted Jay Leno and his audience by bringing exciting animals, such as anacondas, on the show.

Steve's success allowed him and Terri to make some big improvements to Australia Zoo. He was especially proud of the zoo's Animal Planet Crocoseum—a clear water enclosure with ponds and tunnels, allowing visitors to see how crocodiles live and behave in nature. Steve and Terri also expanded their conservation work. In 2002, Steve and Terry expanded their conservation work. They started the Steve Irwin Conservation Foundation to help raise money to save wildlife. This organization was later renamed Wildlife Warriors Worldwide.

Steve died from a stingray wound on September 4, 2006. He was 44 years old. Millions of people around the world were deeply saddened by his death. A large **memorial service** for Steve was held at Australia Zoo. The service was broadcast around the world. Steve's family and friends, along with many of his fans, are continuing his work in wildlife conservation.

WILDLIFE WARRIORS WORLDWIDE

Wildlife Warriors Worldwide is a charity that helps protect injured, threatened, or endangered wildlife. The group has five goals. It aims to protect and improve the environment. It protects threatened or endangered species. Wildlife Warriors carries out nature research and teaches people about animal issues. The group works with other wildlife organizations to help reach their goals, too. Find out more by visiting the Wildlife Warriors Worldwide website at **www.wildlifewarriors.org.au**.

Write a Biography

A person's life story can be the subject of a book. This kind of book is called a biography. Biographies describe the lives of remarkable people, such as those who have achieved great success or have done important things to help others. These people may be alive today or they may have lived many years ago. Reading a biography can help you learn more about a remarkable person.

At school, you might be asked to write a biography. First, decide who you want to write about. You can choose a conservationist, such as Steve Irwin, or any other person you find interesting. Then, find out if your library has any books about this person. Learn as much as you can about him or her. Write down the key events in this person's life. What was this person's childhood like? What has he or she accomplished? What are his or her goals? What makes this person special or unusual?

A concept web is a useful research tool. Read the questions in the following concept web. Answer the questions in your notebook. Your answers will help you write your biography review.

- Where does this individual currently reside?
- Does he or she have a family?

- What did you learn from the books you read in your research?
- Would you suggest these books to others?
- Was anything missing from these books?

- Where and when was this person born?
- Describe his or her parents, siblings, and friends.
- Did this person grow up in unusual circumstances?

Your Opinion

Adulthood

Childhood

WRITING A BIOGRAPHY

Main Accomplishments

Help and Obstacles

Work and Preparation

- What is this person's life's work?
- Has he or she received awards or recognition for accomplishments?
- How have this person's accomplishments served others?

- What was this person's education?
- What was his or her work experience?
- How does this person work; what is or was the process he or she uses or used?

- Did this individual have a positive attitude?
- Did he or she receive help from others?
- Did this person have a mentor?
- Did this person face any hardships?
- If so, how were the hardships overcome?

Timeline

YEAR	STEVE IRWIN	WORLD EVENTS
1962	Steve Irwin is born on February 22.	Rachel Carson writes *Silent Spring*, which starts an environmental movement in the United States.
1971	Nine-year-old Steve captures his first crocodile.	Greenpeace, a worldwide environmental group, is founded in Vancouver, Canada.
1985	The Queensland Government creates the East Coast Crocodile Management Program. Steve volunteers as a crocodile rescuer.	The International Rivers Network is created to protect rivers and communities that depend on them.
1992	Steve marries Terri Raines on June 4. The couple takes over running Australia Zoo.	The Earth Summit is held in Rio de Janerio, Brazil, in June. It is the largest gathering of world leaders in history.
1996	*The Crocodile Hunter* airs in Australia for the first time.	President Bill Clinton names the Grand Staircase-Escalante region of Utah a National Monument.
2004	Steve opens the Australian Wildlife Hospital and Rescue Unit in Queensland.	Wangari Maathai wins the Nobel Peace Prize for her work with the Green Belt Movement.
2006	On September 4, Steve dies from a stingray's barb while swimming off the coast of Queensland, Australia.	Scientists discover more than 100 new species of marine animals in waters near the Hawaiian Islands.

Further Research

How can I find out more about Steve Irwin?

Most libraries have computers that connect to a database for searching for information. If you input a key word, you will be provided with a list of books in the library that contain information on that topic. Non-fiction books are arranged numerically, using their call number. Fiction books are organized alphabetically by the author's last name.

Websites

To learn more about Steve Irwin, visit
www.crocodilehunter.com.au

To learn more about crocodile conservation, visit
www.internationalcrocodilerescue.com.au

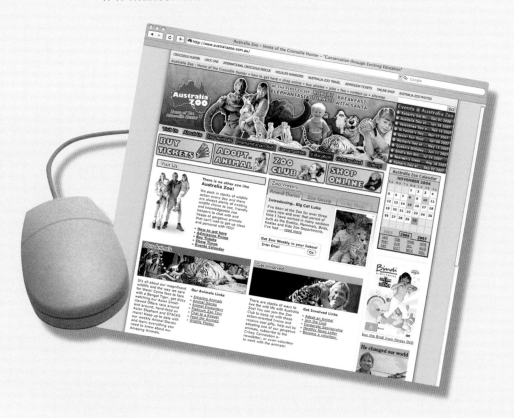

Words to Know

broadcaster: a person who speaks, performs, or presents on a radio or television program

conservation: the protection, improvement, and wise use of natural resources, such as water, plants, and animals, for future generations

deforestation: the destruction of forests

endangered: at risk of being wiped out because of human activities

erosion: wearing away of land or soil by wind, water, or ice

extinct: a species of animal that has ceased to exist

habitat: an animal's natural environment

lobby: to attempt to influence someone to act in a certain way

memorial service: a ceremony marking a person's death

mentor: a wise and trusted teacher

naturalists: people who study nature

preserve: to protect or keep safe

species: a group of living things that have common characteristics

veterinary nurse: someone trained to assist veterinarians, or animal doctors

volunteer: to work for no pay

wildlife sanctuary: land where wildlife can live in safety

Index